GLACIERS ARE ALIVE

Debbie S. Miller · *Illustrated by* Jon Van Zyle

Charlesbridge

SNOWFLAKES whirl and swirl, falling on the high mountains. Inch by inch, the fluffy snow grows deeper and heavier. The snowflakes press against each other and slowly form a sheet of firn ice.

A glacier is born.

Over time, the glacier's ice grows hundreds of feet thick. The belly of the massive glacier crushes the ground, grinds the rock, and plows through the mountains. This giant river of ice carves a valley as it slowly flows toward the sea.

A glacier looks frozen and empty, but it is home to billions of tiny living things.

In summer the days grow longer and warmer. Pink algae blooms on the glacier's surface. The color of this watermelon snow protects the algae from the sun's harsh rays. Squiggly ice worms feed on the algae. A snow bunting snatches a few ice worms for a meal.

As the glacier slowly scoops out the valley, it pushes rocks and dirt along the sides of the mountains, forming massive piles of rocks called a moraine.

With a sudden rush of wings, two small seabirds fly above the moraine. These murrelets spot a slab of granite sheltered by a jumble of boulders. Protected from wind and far from predators, this is a safe place to nest. The mother murrelet lays one precious egg on the cold granite slab.

CRUNCH, CRUSH, CRUNCH, CRUSH.

A brown bear and her three cubs cross the snow-covered glacier. The mother bear leads her cubs from their winter den toward a distant green meadow, where there are plants, flowers, roots, and bulbs to eat.

As the bears plod across the snow, they skirt around the top of a mountain peak that pokes through the glacier. This nunatak is an island of rock in a sea of brilliant ice.

When the glacier slides over steep ground,
the ice cracks and forms deep crevasses.

Two ice climbers carefully pick their way around the crevasses. They wear spiked crampons on their boots for traction, and they are roped together for safety. If one climber slips into a crevasse, the other climber can hammer his ice axe into the glacier and stop his partner from falling.

After many miles the glacier reaches the sea. The face of this enormous tidewater glacier rises twenty stories above the water. But its ice is thicker than that. Much of it hides beneath the water.

A kayaker paddles her boat between floating icebergs. She marvels at the spectacular face of the glacier.

Pinnacles of blue ice lean toward the sea. These seracs look ready to topple and fall.

The kayaker hears the sizzling sound of "bergy seltzer." As the icebergs melt they release air bubbles that pop like fizzy water.

The kayaker also hears the soft COO . . . COOOO of a harbor seal pup calling to its mother as they rest on a floating iceberg. This is a safe birthplace for seals. The huge jigsaw pieces of ice crowding the water make it difficult for predators, such as orcas, to attack.

During the height of summer, warmer temperatures cause the surface of the glacier to melt.

The melting ice brings freshwater rushing into the sea. This water is full of rock flour—minerals from the mountains that the glacier crushed. These minerals help tiny plankton and little fish grow.

CRACK . . .

CRUMBLE . . .

THUNDER . . .

BOOM!

A tower of ice breaks off and topples into the sea. The glacier is calving.

The falling ice churns up the water, bringing plankton and fish to the surface. Hundreds of seabirds dive for fish in the cloudy water, known as glacial milk.

A murrelet's eyes are adapted to seeing through murky conditions. One murrelet dives and zips underwater, then pops up with a silvery fish flapping in its beak.

A tufted puffin runs across the water and takes off. Its huge orange beak is crammed with fish.

Beyond the glacier, sea otters dive for food in the fjord that the powerful river of ice carved long ago. They find clams and mussels on a sill, an old moraine far below the water's surface. The sill provides a good habitat for shellfish, sea stars, and anemones.

At the mouth of the fjord, an enormous creature with huge, wing-like flippers explodes out of the water. The humpback whale crashes back into the sea with a thunderous SPLASH!

Whales are feeding, too, gulping down krill and herring in the fjord. The glacial freshwater and ocean saltwater mix together and create a rich marine environment.

Glacial meltwater helps life flourish, but many glaciers are melting faster than ever before. The earth's temperatures continue to warm because of rapid climate change. With warmer weather, glaciers melt and shrink. Some glaciers are losing so much ice that they will eventually disappear.

Where will the murrelets raise their chicks without tidewater glaciers? Where will these harbor seals have their pups if there are no icebergs?

The murrelets fly above the glacier with their catch. Back home on the rocky moraine, a fluffy chick waits for a meal.

From high mountains to sea, from valley to fjord, from moraine to underwater sill, this powerful river of ice creates a special world where life flourishes.

GLACIERS ARE ALIVE!

AUTHOR'S NOTE

If you fly over Alaska's wilderness, snow-covered mountains and glaciers sweep across the land. There are thousands of glaciers in Alaska. Nearly all of them are losing mass and retreating because of warmer temperatures related to climate change.

Along Alaska's southern coast, there are many tidewater glaciers that extend from the mountains into the sea. In recent years I've explored the world of these coastal glaciers and the abundant life that surrounds them. Kayaking up a fjord to the face of a tidewater glacier was an astonishing and humbling experience. Hiking and camping in magnificent places such as Glacier Bay National Park, Prince William Sound, and Kenai Fjords National Park offered incredible opportunities to witness calving glaciers and see the wildlife that inspired me to write this book. I also had a chance to see glaciers shrinking and no longer reaching the sea.

Many years ago I climbed the beautiful Portage Glacier with ice axe in hand. Surrounded by the Chugach Mountains, I never dreamed that this glacier would slowly melt, retreat, and disappear from our starting point. If I could retrace my footsteps today, I'd be walking on air above a glacial lake. Our glaciers are melting at such a rapid rate that many will disappear within our lifetime.

How does this loss of glacial ice impact our world? The melting of glaciers in Alaska, Canada, Greenland, and Antarctica causes sea levels to rise. This creates challenges for coastal people and animals all over the world. Glaciers and sea ice also reflect sunlight into the atmosphere, which helps to cool our planet. Without glaciers, we would lose that cooling effect, and temperatures would rise even more.

Scientists are studying the impacts of melting glaciers on wildlife. Where will the glacial seals have their pups if there are no icebergs to rest on? How does the increase of glacial freshwater affect ocean life? There are many questions and uncertainties.

One thing that scientists do know is that our planet is experiencing rapid climate change due to human activity. If we switch from fossil fuels to clean, renewable energy; recycle or reuse materials instead of throwing them away; and plant more trees than we cut down, we can help the environment, including the world of glaciers.

What can you, your family, or your class do to help our earth and all living things?

GLOSSARY

bergy seltzer: The sound of air bubbles popping as an iceberg melts. Glacial ice is full of trapped air. As the ice melts, the air bubbles are released and make a fizzy sound like seltzer water.

calving: When slabs and chunks of ice break off the face of a tidewater glacier and fall into the sea.

crevasse: A deep crack or chasm in a glacier. As a thick glacier slowly moves across uneven land, pressure builds within the glacier. This causes the ice to buckle and crack on the surface.

firn ice: Compressed snow that gradually turns into glacial ice. Glaciers are made of many layers of firn ice over thousands of years.

fjord *(also fiord) (fee-ORD)*: A long, narrow inlet or arm of the sea that was carved out by a glacier.

glacial milk: A cream-colored mixture of seawater and tiny particles of rock flour.

krill: A shrimplike crustacean that is an important food for whales, birds, and fish.

moraine: Piles of rock, sand, and dirt that are pushed or carried by a glacier.

murrelet: A small, stout seabird that spends most of its life in the ocean. The murrelet in this book is the Kittlitz's Murrelet, a near-threatened species often seen close to tidewater glaciers.

nunatak *(NUN-uh-tak)*: A mountain peak or pinnacle of rock that is surrounded by glacial ice. *Nunataq* is a Greenlandic Inuit word that means "lonely mountain."

plankton: Small plant and animal organisms that drift with the flow of water currents and tides. Plankton are an important source of food for many animals.

rock flour: Fine particles of mountain rock crushed by a glacier. Also called glacial silt, rock flour is full of minerals and nutrients that mix with water and help life flourish.

serac *(sir-AK)*: A large pinnacle or column of ice on a glacier. Sometimes seracs can be unstable and topple over suddenly.

sill: An underwater moraine formed by a tidewater glacier.

tidewater glacier: A glacier that flows from the mountains into the sea.

To Dean Rand and Megan Ciana, and Tim and Barb Lydon: Thank you for sharing your knowledge of the world of tidewater glaciers in Prince William Sound. And to Stella, who is growing up in this extraordinary glacial world.—D. S. M.

For the children: Glaciers have existed for millions of years, melting, receding, and carving out the land we all live and thrive on today.—J. V. Z.

Special thanks to Louis Sass III, glaciologist and physical scientist with the US Geological Survey, for his invaluable advice and expertise.

Surprise Glacier, a tidewater glacier in Prince William Sound, Alaska. Photograph copyright © Hugh Rose.

Published by Charlesbridge
9 Galen Street, Watertown, MA 02472
(617) 926-0329 · www.charlesbridge.com

Printed in China
(hc) 10 9 8 7 6 5 4 3 2 1

Illustrations done in acrylic on 140-lb. cold-press paper
Display type set in Croteau by Typodermic
Text type set in Londrina by Marcelo Magalhaes
Art digitizing and printing by 1010 Printing International Limited in Huizhou, Guangdong, China
Production supervision by Jennifer Most Delaney
Designed by Diane M. Earley

Library of Congress Cataloging-in-Publication Data
Names: Miller, Debbie S., author. | Van Zyle, Jon, illustrator.
Title: Glaciers are alive / Debbie S. Miller; illustrated by Jon Van Zyle.
Description: Watertown, MA: Charlesbridge, [2023] | Audience: Ages 4–8 years | Audience: Grades 2–3 | Summary: "A glacier may look forbidding and empty, but it provides a rich habitat for animals from the mountains to the sea. As the world's glaciers melt, their disappearance impacts not only the wildlife that calls them home, but also all life on earth. Back matter includes a glossary and an author's note about climate change."—Provided by publisher.
Identifiers: LCCN 2022013895 (print) | LCCN 2022013896 (ebook) | ISBN 9781623543617 (hardcover) | ISBN 9781632893314 (ebook)
Subjects: LCSH: Glaciers—Juvenile literature.
Classification: LCC GB2403.8 .M55 2023 (print) | LCC GB2403.8 (ebook) | DDC 551.31/2—dc23/eng20220922
LC record available at https://lccn.loc.gov/2022013895
LC ebook record available at https://lccn.loc.gov/2022013896